# LOVE'S GREATEST SORROW

Take the Risk or Lose The Chance.
Never Look Back.

## Nelson Wrytings
222

Vue d'asile

Published by Vue d'Asile
Missouri City, Texas

Printed in the United States of America
First Paperback Edition - January 2025

Paperback ISBN: 979-8-218-51735-9

Edited by: Khloe's Thoughts Editing
Cover by: Studio Trid3lpha
Layout by: Make Your Mark Publishing Solutions

# CONTENTS

# ANAGAPESIS

# ACKNOWLEDGEMENTS

I would like to thank the following people and organizations for assisting me with the publishing process for Love's Greatest Sorrow ...

**Self-Publishing Assistant**
Monique Mensah, Make Your Mark Publishing Solutions

**Editing**
Khloe Cain, Khloe's Thoughts Editing

**Cover Design**
Elton Washington, Studio Trid3lpha

**Be**lieve in *be*ing with the only other soul that comprehends your evolving spiritual linguistic prowess, of oneness... *Twin Flame*

*Embrace* if conceivable five months of distance yet unified bliss, unadulterated, a season as you will have, conjures no justifiable timespan. It can *be* the equivalent to dog years or an undaunting "Dory" fish epiphany. A lot can *be* lamented, for instance the original title was once Playlist. Music, previously the binding negotiator to our conundrum in distance. Craving to love her as water like the body lusts hydration too *be*come sovereign. Even purchasing her Frenchie an outfit, so transported by the latent eternal of our union. Yet, she will never understand my complete idiosyncrasies commitment of her. The greatest man I ever knew taught me that is what you love of a person. I felt the hardest open hearted ever over a summer two-third fall, whilst the composition *be*gan to fade for an ambulatory seraph. Remem*be*r the ultimate angel of the most magnificent *be*auty is now the fallen everlasting demon puppeteer. As such was the relationship exquisitely sickening to the audience, but no encore. The echoing image of each, questing for the only other split atom of this universe *Twin Flames* in addiction. Love had no letters, yet possession was the threaded needle. Movements simultaneous, sentences formulated parallel plus just the touch alone was a never experienced strictly plutonic inebriating pleasure. Hours were not timeless, conversations meandered boundlessly fertile, with an anew spark of that birth of her irises and laughter expounding from *be*llies four-dimensional. Saddening, I cannot share the elementary poem written by her and then the subsequent advanced growth into a potential poetess for just I. Alas, all is not meant to *be* shared rather simply stained mentally upon cranial reservoirs. I do not *be*lieve in a wish, and it would *be* a worthless ventured conquest to start the aforementioned. Given the finality in her voice during our last words *be*fore complete extinction, I attempted searching the outside for a breath in hopeless futile *be*lief. Timing could *be* used as the excuse, but time waits for no one! The pureness of breath unquestionable, we were ancient soul lovers. The artist "Common" has a song called "***BE***," the italicize "*be*" throughout represents the first initials of our names. How did a thing, so offering morph lifeless, which gives reasonable pause to the book not having any back pages. There comes a juncture in life's circumstances that should bring about a changing element, one must not look back once more, spawning momentary blindness... *LOVE'S GREATEST SORROW*

*Entombed in my depths I cannot love you, dare not hate you, so I force myself upon secondhand ticks deserting thoughts of you, memoirs of us... to moderately endure breathing...*

# THEORY

Often, catching myself
In thoughts of…
Holding your hand
As we walk side by
Out… of… peripheral
Your smiles, greet the world!
Yet only for I…
As mine for you only…
That stroll in sumptuousness!
I pull you closer…
As though time shall
Stand motionless for
An eternity's interlude in extravagance…
The inviting pause of soft exhale elations
Inhales of security
Embracing what was…
Understood almost two decades ago.
In glossy iris reserves
That dared not speak…
Past circumstances
Yes, time has seasonal winds.
As uttered by you recently
Now, now we *be*long here.
Deserve this space!
Crave the shielding of…
Hearts aware
Mentally clear

Continued…

Spiritually listening
Hearing what the universe
Must pronounce…
All we must do…
Is emit the will willingly.
And that will… shall *be* given.
Unequivocally
Sooo let us,
Mature euphorically
Growing youthful together…

# PERMISSION OF MORNS ARRIVAL

Can I suspend...
Upon your every elocution
Until the wee hours
Amongst the stars
Kissing each shoulder, eyes closed.
Feeling your body tingle
Then investigate,
Tainted portals seeking neverland.
Asking for twinkling's
That peer *be*yond time
Seek your cold,
Until warm yearns
The breeze... touching your hair.
Collide with my spirit!
Until am*be*rs correlate
To replenish the earth's core...
Upon sandy barefoot *be*aches
That hydrate tootsies...
Dancing in natural salty bubbles
Love us unadulterated...
Inebriated even... from the spiritual realm,
Whilst pursuing life...

# INITIAL PROMINENCE

Smoldering within us
At the edge of
Realities firmament...
I... I could share,
That I hope oddly to *be*lieve
More this time...
Yet... I would rather *F*eel.
The touch of visions
Her presence balances,
Calm exterior
Though my heart races
As woman she implores
That I slow down...
As man
Exuding the patience
That attracted her,
Yet, we are now free!
In this season
Clutching our interlocked fist...
As a strand of pearls
Hovering in surprise
Excessively to our...
Next destination
After breakfast
Levitating in quest
For the time of first, firsts

Continued...

We are ours...
No middle separation
Adjoining alignment
Of position
Time has already told...
On itself
Forever
For always
For love...

# AS EQUALS

Remem*be*ring the initial flame
Kindling amongst
Her window pains once... more...
The restorative smile
*Be*queathed *be*auty unto
The inhabitants
In her sanctuaries
We sought through
The pieces of wreckage
Within decades
Of decay...
I'll give you
The bounty of piracy
Live too Love the Lust
Of untold fortunes
The power within
Just your digit pinky
Shall *be* endless
Or the opposite...
The saying goes
No one man or woman
For that matter
Should have all that power
That is *be*cause
It should *be*
Man, equal with Woman
Of sovereignty...

To my Empress...

# TWIN FLAME INVITATION

My valves…
In reception of yours…
Resuscitation of my own
Body thrusting for your cells…
Spirit in detection of your you…
Mental's vertical
At the fringe
Ready to base jump
In oneness parachute-less
Yet it *be* my soul.
That seeks the
Intertwining of our atoms
Amongst the
Known then unknown,
COSMOS
*Come With…*

# SEARCH FOR VIBRATION

Habitually racing to you
Amongst the
White noise confusion
It is us
In the motionlessness...
That softens
The hardened crust
For... each
Cannot say it's you
Enough while leering
Nestled in the considerate
Cozying to the case of compassion
That I shall hold
You as mine
Protecting every inch
Of your everything
Yes, my Empress...
Everything throughout
Our last breath
For time has shown
Itself to *be* truly
Graceful of the nature in
One must go through life
To get to more than just
Living...

# WEATHER

On this day of
Overshadowing forecast
The picture of you
Stored within
Memory banks
Provides rays of preserved
Sunshine that forge
Spirit too...
Communicate with soul
Yielding an upward curl
Upon my facial corners
That shall forever
Only touch yours
For you are the Sun
*Be*sos y *Be*sos...

# SAVAGERY

Lying stark-naked
As namesakes
Adam & Eve
*Be*fore the fruit
Of forbidden-ness
Was lip rimmed
Teeth penetrating
In exploration...
Dating some, though
It seems millenniums
Of scars highlander-*ish*
For this is
One of the rarest
Mathematical equations
When two human souls can
Morph into
There can *be* only one
Vital *be*ing...

# PRISM

Of your wakened words
To my core
Your tutelage is astounding
Patiently adoring
The potential of each rise
Of love... with...
Every prism molecule
Present particle
You birth
The elevated level
Of mental stability
Physical healing
Spiritual enlightenment
Coherent awareness
I remember us...
Captured in this specific embrace...
Of your splendor
From eras ancient
In the present-day
Unto our future
My Love...
Let us trust each other
Enough to recognize
More admiration about we...

# UNSUSPECTING

The elegance with which
Left handedly you
Share the line of
Outer forearm
To elbow then
Feminine sculpted bicep appears
As the graceful gathering
Of strands to *be* situated
Across shoulder
Tickling your back lightly
Now arranging
Upon left upper breast
From your tiny fingertip
That now caress your cheek
Is an artform
Free of deception…
Meticulous in movements
*Be*ckoning lost souls
I am found…
Inhaling the air
Of apprehension
My Empress…

# SERENDIPITOUS

Slum*ber* is…
Near impossible
After communing
Evolving hardest
Wanting to comeback
Earth down
What *be* this feeling of
Metaphorical head
Of outer body unaltered
Plagiarized pleasures
As a feeling in synchronized selves
Shall we leave
Gratuitous amounts
Of invoked
Debaucherous natures
In abundance
Li*be*rally extract
Sapiosexual intellects
Physical thought after
Amid dialects
That only we comprehend

# VULNERABLE

Longitude of…
Potentially falling tears no longer
Feel load *be*aring…
Can I, now possibly fathom
The… sob without
The… not turning
In front of woman
When water need *be* displaced…
As a male
Tired of the world stressed
Again, theoretically not hold head
To lowing position
*Be*ing petrified, penetrable even…
*THANK YOU*, for the
Emotions of genuineness

One would think the aching heart of pain hurts worse, wait
until the Fahrenheit of love singes your pores…

# MISSING HER

In my exhaustion of
Marginally saddened sensitivity
I felt you remotely console me
For, for a moment I scraped
A thing of your past by
Just a wording glance…
Triggering a past-present
Deep seeded distaste…
Whilst setting **be**dside
Feet firmly planted
Head gently slumped
The paranormal weight I categorically desired
Pressed against me skin to skin
Your soul whispered
I'm ok my love, my love we are more
Through spiritual connection
You confirmed that energy transfer
Verbally the next day…
Your enhanced minute soliloquy felt like
Stout yet soft trumpet in drum
As your armed hand
Strummed across my chest…
The brilliance
In your cunning tongue
Erased my insecurities
As hu-man **be**ing
For fear of fear

Continued…

Provides motivated lostness
Yet, you sought
Elongated loneliness
Heart mine incapable of
Un or intentional mistreatment
Of your refinement
Every thought
Honors you…
Basorexia

# CONCISENESS

The decision has *be*en consumed
To halt the ascension for air
Levitation holds its position purpose
For so we are now
Perpetually self-sustaining
Pollutants have *be*en entirely
Dispelled from hemispheres
Representing us as the purified plural
Perimeter of completion
Our love is effervescence
Once drowning within three counts
Captivating we *be*hold
In each other's irises
Supplying sustenance that
Shall fulfill ecologies
Within millenniums
We thrive in factual
Fashion of procreation
Destin to surmount
Further worldly than
What a mental can breach
Yonder than what
Pupils can aspire
Meager cranium enclosures
Shall perish questing
Our plight in the
Attempt at a slight grasp

Continued...

As they grapple in adolescence
The bond that wraps us
Limitless of momentum
Calibration unquantifiable
To the last present inhale

I could not resist, you ok ba*be*!

# ACKNOWLEDGEMENT

This sensation
Is as of neonatal
Fresh from womb…
In this novel quality arrangement
The look for reassurance
Moves about the mind
I need not
Question replenishment
Yet, relations call
Like bosom
To mouth
Through veracity
In panicked nourish filled rants
Suckling wet membrane
Aching traverses the physique…
Could the statement
Of a woman
*Be*ing Mother Earth
Foster untold validity…
Does she feel
The pull of
A Father's protection
To *be* graced
Within a presence
*Be*yond truth in conception
What say us…
For I lay amazed

# MANO Y MANO

Poised amongst
Her promotions
Brings about
Reasons to live
In conjunction
The juxtaposition of
Intercourse *be* the
Fore afterthought
Subtleness of my eyes rolls across
The unchartered authenticity
However, it is the chartered
Comprised of unhurried swallows
Of non-detainment
Expressive explosion
Fingertips offering her breaths pause
She knew never
The contained limitless serenity
Of in her own skin.
Til this quadrant
That protection
Within an
Unconditional embrace
Two hands
Making love
Palm to palm
Radiating energy throughout

Continued...

Bodies unconscious flow drowsy
Like tiny magnets
Representing caged hearts
Uniting the vital-*be*ing...

# FYRE

Sorry is used by
The non-honest
Thank you does
Not spew from loves lips
Of any climate
Fahrenheit or Celsius
I shall stoke your coals
Almost to incineration
However, never a promise, though
Constantly of my words...

# ALL OF ME, ALL OF YOU

Everything of me
In its singular form
*Be* justifiably flawed
In recognition
Of this very tick
I've walked in places
Seen things
However, experienced
Lesser amounts
In breaths that I
Should never have
Inhaled to exhaled
That existence
No longer an observation
Steps of future
With mere thoughts
Of only your hand…
That award
I only want
To inhale
Your essence
In moments
That have yet
To blossom
The immaculate blooms
Of conversing

Continued…

Within your
Iris am**be**rs
Passionate lyrics
The totality of warmth
Hints in anticipation
Dance with me
Minds at li**be**rty
In the simplicity
**Be**fore us
Just kiss me
With our mental
Rational unguarded...

# PREMATURE

Blamelessly unclothed of
Penetrating contemplations
In the bated-ness of aggressions...
Fondling your
Eve descendent worthiness
With irises
In hours
To prepare
For what's to cum
Ba*be* it's...
Hella hard
While *be*ing stout
To contain
My cream
*Be*gging to
Spray your fortifications
Then emanate
The first time
Of you *be*ing
My first last all eternal
I may have
To succumb...
Enveloped by your aqueous
To minute man status
For this moment
Barring the occasional quickie
As though high

Continued...

From releasing pheromones
Like ashes
Rising Phoenix
Frightening as that may *be*
We are each other's trophies
This keenness is…
Killing me smalls lol (a quim of hers)

# THIRST

Indulgences **be**
To drink of you
Upon moon**be**ams
That bless the
Furthest mountain hidden
Your spirit resides
Frolicking amongst
Cloud formations
I only want
To taste of you
Upon salty
Sea shores
Warm sands
At tide peaks
Drown me of
Your everlasting substances
Flesh unbound
I only see
Your soul
As you see mine
Gracefully flourishing
Souls united
You are the
Only adversary
Thought worthy…

# GIVE PAUSE

Need doth your skin
To memorize
My fingerprints
Glance to glance
As mine ears
To your *be*ating
Heart as ours
Line for line
You, you
The ONLY spirit
Capable of understanding
This me through
Nonverbal expressions
Whichever of us noted
I, trembled as tongues tied
Healthily within your
Extremities insnared smooch…
Unadulteratedly
Defenseless in
Undertakings
Hither never *be*en
You as you are too I
Of simultaneousness
This now the imminent
Precession *be*yond
The weeds
Complex doctorate initiation

Continued…

Forever unending commingling
Our soul's soil
Now spiritual
Sovereign asylum
Foreign flesh to all
Yet, most familiar
Finally, the knowledge
Of how to love, *be* love…

# NIGHTS

Matter not
The verse
A Moon
Is just simply
The night
Sun...

# REFLECTION

My own hands
No longer
**Be**long to
The yearn that
Once crisscrossed aimlessly
As seconds
**Be**gan expansion
Our ships…
Set course
As two trains
Potentially colliding
Upon same track
I **be**came yours
For only the
Graceful delicate touch
Of your emulating hands
Can unequivocally fulfill
The erection of time

# THIS ONE BABE

Heart**beat** **be**
Distinctively different
Now feeling the second
One pulse combined
So faintly kissing
Yet firmly significant
Unto our constellations
Diagonally my continents
Once recklessness
Awareness morphing
Unabandon concisely
Understanding inception
Scientific exploration
To explain this
Euphoric feeling to miniature…
Words need not **be**
For every cell
Is pondering
Its inceptive birth…
As the **bee**
Pollinates the flower
A wave is rising
At all times
You are the womb
That nurtures…
I shield of protection…
Scouring the veiled
Identified nonentities

# MY ONLY FIX

Through the years
Her psyche
Hasn't blinded
Tainted is such a world
That we live
Yet circumstances
Had not left
Her enough scorned
Of pain's past...
As a mythical
Above its own fragmented
Aura of energy
Cleansing voice
Spirit humble
Still pure as a dove
She can barely
Remem**ber** seasons
When winter
Covered life
As summer...
Then the two
Merely reversing
Temperatures...
Void once existed and now
Focusing peace shimmers
Safeguarding her temples
Joyous the smile

Continued...

That resonates…
Residing upon face
Such the *be*autiful elixirs
The addiction that
One shall only
Dream to live

# OSCULATION

As idioms ballet
Fervor oblique in
Annealed orifices
Like polliwogs
Pooling the ambition of
Pleasure-seeking covets
In the temperateness of a July…
Nonetheless still encompassing
Lovers unriddled supplementary…
The likings of
Silhouettes sailplaning about
Minds in fluently infusions
Taking the high sentry
To nucha then occipital
Also lower at mid lumbar
The scapula's involuntarily
Contort by palmar
Carpus tie in offering
As knees lock
Trying to get in
Another layer
Finally standing
At the edge
We leap…
Dramatically smitten

# FREAKS OF NATURE

Songbird humans
Are far often
Overly exerted…
Wings well strained
In youth
Vocals stifled…
Her irises
Spoke with tears
Supplying rivers
I sipped from long ago
Desperately hydrating
My spirit depraved had…
Had *be*en drained
Her soul's voice
As well petrified
So, we were amicable
To familiarize
Selves of new oxygen
Upon my reentry
Her agreeance
The first time
Should only *be*
Universal hemispheric
*Haiku Equations*
*"Mentally it was*
*I that could not infiltrate*
*Her prematurely"*

Continued…

We owned that interstellar
To this day standing
As underpinning

# DEBTORS SOUL

Imperfect as indy's
Coupling perfection
Hmmmmmm
Surely, I would
Disintegrate without
Her laughter
With portraiture
*Be*aming astronomically...
I Moonlight fueling Her Sun
Circumference rotations
She is intelligence...
To have potentially
Never known her
Like as such
Would have *be*en a life
Fractured in shadowed darknesses
Which I once craved
However immeasurable is
Her Sistine...
Imploring I to her light
Calculated in distances
Driven too spiritually
Cultivate her as vineyard
Then nibble of
The fruits while laboring
Once forbidden nevermore...

Continued...

Hence forth
Now moistly ripened,
For the supple pluck…
Living upon her statues
Time now due…

# GENUINELY SPEAKING

Love in its purity
*Be* not a thing you unearth
Yet, an island
With gravitational pulleys
Marionetting your
Inner self smoothly parallel
To the banshee
Seeking its prey
For inevitably love
Warrants the lusts of death...
Timeless in its duel
Sprinting in a stratums
Inebriated enervations
*Be*ckoning lawless laughter
Deeply hidden within *be*llies
Of the freshest cuisines
Awaiting dinner service
Amongst 21 courses
Priceless *be* the tasty
Gratuitous served bill
Morsels so so so ominous
Representing the exacting
Pleasantries that exist
About the silver platter of pain
Forecast like the box
Of pagan Christmas delectables

Continued...

Each bite slightly
Apprehensive in warning labels
Of misread details
Tweaking for each ingestion

# FORETHOUGHTS

The brain of nothing
Knows not *be*lief
Clinging to hope
This barren wasteland
That has led...
A many astray
From destinies destination
Of two creating one
The math is possible
Potentially we all
Derail in mass media
Initially listening to picture boxes
"War of the Worlds"
Consuming gluttonous natures
Sex, drugs, music waring religions
Oaths are not as royal
As we have *be*en
Herded to *be*lieve
Traces of us
Gallup about
In desolation
Seek home's heart
Suffocating compartments
Crying upon deaf
Drums *be*ating to strike
Within passion
Trapped along

Continued...

Forgottenness pleading
Reprieves that shall
Never potentially emerge
Is it ever too late?
To conceptualize recoil

# REAL ESTATE

That wanting visualization of land
Where only we can respire
Deserted isles that lovers apprehend
Enthralled within selfness
Specks of sands
From taught genetic isolation
Supplanted from elders' views
By rite of choice nonconventional
Alone yet not lonely
Surrounded by
Warm even days
The odd nights coolness
Enhanced by engulfing seas
Excepting excrement
As fertilization
With largest elephant ears
Waterfalls that come
In toppling motions
Amongst another
Upon trickled trembles
Might we explore
Misty abstract notions
Transforming iridescent glimmerings
Where after derives
Consecrated impression
To intoxications
Invoking obsessed cheerfulness
That romp from dependently
Cohesive meditations

# COOL OUTSIDE, HOT MIDDLE

Though nothing can buffer us from life
Having *Loved* will suffice in death
The truth of the **be**ginning...
We're all matter
Plus, matter
At ending
Voyage

# LESS GENDER

The contest is to amplify
**Being** of love
That rarest microclimate
Yonder further than what
One views as the heavens
For everyone loves
The haven that is of **be**ing loved
To **be** regarded undyingly
Caresses interweaving crevices
Thoughts so unyielding
Stepping just to the point of noxiousness
That appalls surrounding spectators
Right where work shall
Almost not **be** processed
Yet, carries on
So, what is love
Forward cliché banter
Love is a tiny extinction
The French have a phrase
"La Petite Mort"
"The Little Death"
As I understand
Love as ceaseless energy
Emergent from engrossed
Scorching cauldrons of revulsion
That only one purified love
Shall balance telepathically

Continued...

Faithfully interlocking
Mental collectives
To the calm of mysteries
Enlightening internal dimness

# AT THIS VERY MOMENT

Eager to choke
Bias tainted
On your everything
For the rest of
Unanticipated galaxies

# ELEUTHERIA (LENNY KRAVITZ)

If… this we
**Be** a phase
Allow the spark multi
To **be** interminable
Incurable facet
Let it **be** the
Treacliest pungent ingredients
Of creation
Feasibly desirous
When it comes to us
Thoroughly selfish
Give this vibration
The timeless tune
Yield disappearance
Absent of heart
In starburst
That kerosene our way
Spiritual guidance
Pause not one
Urge of thought
As to not bind
Or blind sight
Excepting life
For our perfect lessness
That it is
For promises
**Be** a flawed pitfall

Continued...

Not worthy
For life
Cannot *be* compared
To a game
We *be* not the foot race
Yet, we are ascension
Atmospherically tangible

# WHAT HAPPENS STAYS

Encountering the lone
Affection of all
Periods in the
City of superficial sinners
Flaccid from
The whole shebang
Dissecting her
Out intakes
For the rest
Of a perpetuity black hole
We shall only
Gravitate unified
Our nations
Infinitely combined
Time compressed
Itself filled cheekiness
Playful swag
Augmented zeal
Of mixed florae's
Competitively aggressive
Freakishly gleeful
Nonsexual enrichment
Forged palpitations
In imprudence the hunt
Has shuffled
To the inexplicable
Madness of method
Shall we *be* saints…

# CONCISENESS

Understanding…
The decadence of sweet
Was never known
Until your lips *be*came mine…
When realm rest activates
Thoughts of you
Are more profoundly noticeable
Which is why
Words need not *be* slated
At whatever status
Of conscious…
Internal communication
*Be* divinely concise
If I could simplify
Saying the words
I love you… I'm in love
With only you
No other *be*ing exist
I would
Yet, we have
On such a primal level
For energy cannot
*Be* destroyed
Therefore, our ambiences
Have collectively imprinted
Amongst themselves

Continued…

Consistently coherent
How the words must
*Be* spoken with
Quintessential connotation...

# CUDDLE

My love, let us practice
Absolutely dress rehearse… on *be*ing
Involuntarily intimate
If we are to procure
Any degree of perfection
From our imperfections
Allow our subconscious
To meld, as one
For without that highest peace…
One shall not
Achieve epicenter
Within… that mind
The cognizant
Is merely
A figment of
Worldly imagination…
Leaves consumed by winds
Destination less dreams…
Rarely take form
Void disciplines
My softest circumference ever
Which only
Your touch shapes this misshapen vessel
As clay
Mold me of your enhanced
Patterns of thought

Continued…

And I shall complete the same
For we are the learned
Last stand
Which is in relief
Ultimately our commencement…

# THE LOVE OF YOU

Quantifiable measurement...
The why in *be*ing
In love about you...

# MOTIVE

The reason, bias origin
To… love… us
To… love… us
To… love… us
We are we
Individual lucidity
Of finely aged infancy
Affording us that power
Plus, sheer force
*Be* strength
Soul, heart, mind
Singular intensified life-force
Enough to never wilt
As plurals
When faced with adversity
What is an impediment
Lover…
To… love… us

# SUCCULENT

Flesh is to *be* devoured ferociously
Plants consumed of patience
We shall *be* methodically more of both
Carnivorously vegan
Mmmmhmmmm

# THIRD EYE

To **be** just
In love with you
Is minuscule in thought
You understand
What is said
Of tiny minds...
Grandeur is the
Pulpit of aspiration
One's bureau must **be**
Designed fortuitousness
We are of
The Most High
And as such...
Closed eyes shall
See faith clearly
Walking with conviction
About the world
Allowing no nothing
Falsehood type incisions
For there is no
Piercing laceration
Unhealable of our Amalgamation...

# PHOTOSYNTHESIS

Blades of grass
Send breezily tickle invites
To the soft under*be*lly
Of flowers to openly laugh
With designated rays and dance about…
Jazzy within morning's dew
Whilst pedals
Sip hydration rolling
To its pistil
Stems stand at devotion
In reach of bluest skies…
Welcoming insects
Cross pollination
Stationary within
Fertile soil
Roots conjoin at the depths
Of dark deepened nourishment
The process
*Be* defiance in a world
Aimed too unalive
The forest *be*yond the trees
At the fall of dusk
NICU seedlings
Permeate the upper crust
Sprouting delightedly
At the starry night
Excited to *be* the

Continued...

Tallest in days to come...
Espousal the soon now
Forever only last
The certain length...

# EDIFICATION

I'd teach
The world to write
Once again
That brilliance
On the acceptable imperfections
That make us whole
In elucidations
Kept hidden
Vulnerable variances dwelling
Making us more
More worthy of alternative
Why present
Shallow shortcomings
When the truth
Of our souls
Clamor bursting at the seams
In search
Of nothing less
Than an equal
Odd is the landmass
You've placed self upon
Imploring permission
To come aboard
Setting sail forward
Without compass
Until the misunderstood

Continued...

Solomon's plight is
Situated within the grasp
Of a subsequent
Juvenile elderly gaze…

# REBIRTH

Me looking at us
Each time as though
It is the initial...
Utterly surprised
At what shall materialize

# SPECTACLE

Frequently...
The jolt to hear
Your voice...
Nestled in the comforts
Of tones
The fluctuations
In the not so
Graceful imbalance
Intrigues my heart...
When did I **be**come
So ruptured
In the warmth
Of our vessels
That space
Drooling to
Smell your waking
After essence pheromones
Love is such a thing
Love... is... such a miracle
Love has **be**come... such a phenomenon

# NEVER FINISHED

Catch me
I've fallen
Ba*be,* I can
Feel your heart
*Be*ating as shadow
In the hull
Of my ticker
Time once
Ran from us
Past illusions
Now we walk
Together as a spell
Plagiarizing
My mind
To write
Poems these
Not only exist
For our
Flesh worldly
Yet, in selfishness
We share
Take me
Take me
Back to
Your divine
Might we *be*
Cupid wasted

Continued...

Facing embraces
Of coitus faces
That pre-droll
Mixed fragrances
Wetting sheets
Less *be* speech
More most of
Heaviest inaudible exhaustions
From proverbial mouths
Awwww ba*be*
I'm still looking
*Be*twixt catatonic
Of that intimate space
We can *be* more exposed...

# PROSPECT

In years to come
I prefer contemplation
Directly into with
Your eyes on all days
A testimony at the
Level of opulence
Achieved plus
That we shall...
For we, we
Are more than
What can *be*
Imaged of love...

Actions promise nothing...

# IN DECADES

Will she ever
Understand that
I was never
Afraid of her
Dying first
But it **be**
The internal
Of what shall
Cease living
Within me
After her last
Breath just
**Be**fore death…

Success is not perception but action…

# FLAIR

Time is the endowment
That we should
Want the need to unclutter
Simplistically together incessantly...

# KINGDOMS

This temple is poetry
The Creator's creation
Solitude of mental health
Establishment of commerce
Diverse gestures
Of crucial natures striking
That grin at the *be*witching hour
Entranced possessions
Harmonizing enchanted hues
That only ancient's voyage…
This thread invisible to the common
One need not see
What does not pertain to them
For it *be*longs to us
That is all that shall *be* articulated

# ENTHUSIASTIC

That excitement
Captured within your voice
The unexpected invitation
In doing something you've wanted
My innate intuition
A spontaneous request

# FOREIGN FEEL

Always baffling
When I say
I'm with the love,
Of life's expectancy
For people
Retort surely
You've *be*en in love…
Previous to this moment
I acknowledged nothing.
Of temporary conquest
For this uniqueness
I am conquered.

# SUSPICION

What it is
To never think of another!
Fathom the appetite!
Having not any epiphany
Of drifting with
Anyone other
Desiring the intimate release
With split offset exclusively
Then you will know
Absolute love
For a lot can *be* true
Clinch the evidence in
Giving yourself unified
Then you shall have
Entered wisdom.
Fulfilling knowledge
Reflected equal foreseen.
Both cham*be*ring selves
Within the universe
As Binary Stars...

# (864,000 SECONDS)

20.798363° N, 156.3311924° W

You are….
Going to possibly ponder
When back…
He's too quiet.
It's just *be*en lengthy.
I haven't heard your voice.
More so able to listen…
At duration within the
Symphonic endurance
The sounds of your vocals…
Just as picturesque
As the views you've
Encompassed while on hiatus.
That offer shock value.
Pushing only ones
Faith to worship.
Can you hear?
The enchantment
Of my nucleus
Catatonic at the
Closer distance of space
Sympathetic fluctuation
There's something
About that paradise
To *be* enjoyed
Within the cheer

Continued...

Of your vocal cords
Highs then lows,
Gravity filled Hawaiian horizons
Realities of your knowns, my unknowns
For what are words?
To the sightless
Yet, the eyes of the present
All just to say.
Your voice is without question…
*Be* needed to fuel the essentials
You are exponentially missed…
My love is still only more yours …

# ANAGAPESIS

**(n.) loss of feelings for someone who was formerly loved, falling out of love.**

*"Thank you for the tragedy. I need it for my art."*
~Kurt Cobain~

# MOON & THE SKY (SADE)

Calling in the voice of
Finality null discussion
Sentences were...
Structured rhetorical...
Cold causing moisture
From lungs
And... just like that
YOU laid me down and left me...
For the alliance of lions
To unleash the *LYCAN*...

# PANIC

I could not
Eat for 3 days!
Barely breathing,
When she partially
Began to entirely pry…
Her hearts
Separation from mine…
Almost alone again…
Never lonely
For the greatest
Lover I shall
Ever experience,
In this lifetime
Are… WORDS
As we understand each
This pure LOVE which…
I embrace my…
Little numerous deaths
As they birth
Customarily having visions
Of time stamps
Yet, this was spell blinded…
In owning self-pity meditation of pain
I… never anything
So openly much
Free of all qualms
In not being judged

Continued…

Unselfishly of complete movement
Motion forward
So, I dreamt…
Not one for hoping.
I believe in the finality,
Of this death
Rising In Peace
Abruptly upon another
Conundrums horizon…


She once offered me a thing, that I hadn't believed in for 2 decades and before I could blink, took it away.

"Hope, let me tell you something, my friend. Hope is a DANGEROUS thing. HOPE can drive a <u>MAN</u> insane; it's got no use on the inside. You'd better get used to that idea." Ellis Boyd - Red… The Shawshank Redemption

Our world is just a bigger inside!

# CELL THERAPY

I've… had to
Peel body
Out of chairs
From bed coverings
Like silken ensnared insect…
Alone not lonely again
Yet, deteriorating warmth…
Blood of life flowing…
From lacerations
By lover's tongue
I would ask why?
Futile that would be!
How does…
A soul… not grimace…
At the desolation as it
Consumes crippling thought…
By the tenth of a second
I still love…
The air
But can scarcely
Stand it at the same…
The diminished whiffs of rancidness
Us decaying rapidly…
Time, one shall never
Underestimate what it holds…
Which for us… crematorium

# JEJUNE

I guess if,
I knew why…
You rushed your departure…
We would be,
In each's present
Long distance…
Grasping for patterns
Granting less shelter
I walked over,
A bridge
And the winds
Echoed the word.
"jump" softly
In lowercase letters
I'd managed the time,
Finding sleepless morning
To type your personal
Book of poetry…
Louder anticipation "JUMP…"
Screaming to
See you!
I had to explain.
To all of them
But they refused.
To understand.
As infants do
*The Collective…*

Continued…

In conjoining unrest
Searching for...
The severed Bifrost
Leaving the one
Inconsolable persona
So, to be buried
For that one...
Could drown us all...
They mentally unalive one
In saving the sum

# TURMOIL

How many pieces
Need be written.
Before self-anointing Authorship...
In publishing response
Does our mortality
Deserve equal billing...
Do works of
Accumulated displeasures
Account for... more less...
Concisely shown.
No longer slightly tolerably pleasing...
Does rubbish
Seize the why!
Once it has become discardable
Drifting... aimless... mental
As many as it takes
To the last of my last...
I shall stand again in singular brilliance

# ACKNOWLEDGEMENT

I be the fortunate human,
That becomes…
Broken by disillusion!
Nevermore entrusting
Another with this heart…
However, not the sole owner…
Parchment on the other hand
For each outcome
Offers the same,
Yearning of solution
For paper love lusts the pen…
Within my inclusion
Do I need speech therapy…
Whom shall save,
The soulless
For solitude
Is the apparent
Healer of all atoms
I've lived several,
Destinies of unraveling…
Who can I run to…
But self
When I need
Loves enchanting physical graces…
The riposte
For I am at my best worst
Loving only myself

Continued…

The most positive
Motivating force
Of my life
I must roam…

# SPEECHLESS

A kiss so deeply paralyzing.
I had on no occasion felt previously
A touch that
I assumed... loves...
Me back unbiased as I almost
Misconstrued the simultaneous
Heartbeat instantaneously...
Faintest palpitations were clarified.
They can mature frostbitten...
Leave you,
Just slightly
Able to endure.
The eye opening
Effects of life's
Excruciating discombobulation...
Challenging to reconcile
And maybe not...
With self-embarrassment
Time after time...
Should I view the rest,
As objects significantly
In this next
Finally come to grips with the word.
Objectification as recognizable
Being possibly acceptable...
Upon intrusive relations
After half a century

Continued...

My strains astonished…
More after self
Assessment of 30 years
Struggling with the
Species that is opposite
Attracted still…
I've always revered as equal.
But been treated less to them,
On the over-under…

# PLAYLIST

The collaborative title
Of our season
Co-writing each other
Plural once
In thoughts of revelation…
Grandeur that was to withstand…
Infantile was universe so, so fragile.
Shall we ever be?
"Minds as one"
Beyond platonic
Awkwardness does either
Collectives possess,
The yielding courage
Of recoil the worthy listen
Before time dodges space
At winds surreal
As it would seem
Beckoning hearts
To be in love?
Regardless of circumstances
Configurational logistics
Like countless films
As they were created…
For life imitates art
Producing conclusion
Of the initially
Aforementioned

Continued…

Could we goad…
A reason for belief
I love you…
As we return to atoms
In pursuit of next lifetime…
Further than the infinite cosmos


"Only once the drugs are gone, I feel like dying, I feel like crying…" Lil Wayne

This was the original title of the book. Songs had this thing of expansion for us within the once carrying foggy distant. The shame exists, of the changing of the flow and then not. And so, it goes when the music stops. The last Playlist I offered her, was at 20.798363° N, 156.3311924° W. There was no reply, and no exchange of communication remains…

# FINAL PLAYLIST 15 SONGS, 55 MINUTES

2003 Prototype - Outkast

2020 Catastrophic – Eric Penn

2011 The Moon and the Sky (Remix) [feat. JAY-Z] -SADE

2007 Ready for Love – Luther Vandross

2018 Shallow – Lady Gaga & Bradly Cooper

1997 Searching (Live) – Erykah Badu

2014 Stay With Me – Sam Smith

2023 Make believe (acoustic) – Elijah Woods

2022 Sad Love - Whitney Woerz

2011 Set Fire to the Rain – Adele

2018 Someone You Loved – Lewis Capaldi

2023 Some Things I'll Never Know – Teddy Swims

2018 Consequences – Camila Cabello

2023 Vampire – Olivia Rodrigo

2017 Redbone Smooth Jazz All Stars Cover – Childish Gambino

1984 Careless Whisper – George Michael

*2019 – Fly Again – Slowed by Lil Chris Kevin Gates

# CLIMAX OF HYPER-INDEPENDENCE

the.offbeat.therapist

She was the... at dawn,
Dew dream of hydration...
I, the pedal...
Just as the
Sun was rolling.
From the attraction of opposite
Pre-dehydration launched...
Yet, limbs continuously
Protruded... for her as sky...
At the height of highest noon
Sunrise, she did... scorch
I dripped precipitation...
As the rotation
Slowed axis exuberance.
In failed attempt
At halting the Moon
Weakness rendered.
Forging hibernation
To forcefully appropriate back
Extremist control...
I quietly beseeched.
Once... More... Reprieve...
To no avail...

Continued...

Missing one last
Dance under the moonlight.

The manner in which you operate words establishes precedence...
*Hyper-Independence* - the.offbeat.therapist - Instagram

# DARKNESS AMONGST LIGHT

If I had belief in a wish,
It would be to not
Have a photographic
Memory only for this…
The precision in which
Genuinely we affixed fixated…
The freakishly reflective properties
How our elbows had
A way about them.
A kiss of ultimately
Delicate provoked passions
Intellectual synopses
Contacted fyre stimuli
The lover…
Of my collective
Has been ironed masked
Without doppelganger,
Stretching for
Day Modern Rapunzel's
Refusal to relinquish.
The shelter of mane
From the notion of chivalry
For what woman
Craves a Knight these days
Not to save her from title
However, the kindness
Of masculine natures

Continued…

Now as one of the
Kings of all my sorrows
I shall defend.
Under lock and key
Unnerved essence
Amongst debauchery
For its embattled status
Presents stifling inclusions…
Surely my demons
Shall exult the return of anew.
***ENTHUSIASTICALLY VIGOROUS…***
*For I coitus'd myself…*


*And then the voice of virtue that offers one patience spoke…*
*"Quiet Your Mind…"*

# COUPLE OF FOREVERS...

For what of life
If loss, did not exist
But lost...
I reached for you
With none return.
Yet, your yield
Is unquestionably
Unquantifiable...
Tears stream hydrogen,
As my heart burns
In the ruins
Of this Phoenix,
Atmospheric pressure
Shalt never fold
The glory of existences
That few shall hold
Not one thing be
Comparable to us
The love extraordinary
Oxygen the quality
Of delicacy
I have become
Learned that everything
Is bearable in nature.
Through grace
You shared...

Continued...

Spare me not
One moment
Of nothing
That be everything...
In this stillness
That pauses, yet pushes
Movements yonder
Beyond success...
In serendipitous solidarity
The beginning...

# ABOUT THE AUTHOR

**NELSON WRYTINGS** hails from Houston, TX, embodying a unique blend of southern charm and international perspective. With over thirty years of writing experience, he weaves together the knowledge and insights gained from his travels to create a distinctive literary voice. Beyond crafting poetry that speaks to the intellectual soul, Wrytings indulges in his passions for collecting antique typewriters and rediscovering forgotten vinyl classics. His greatest love is the written word, and he treasures its power to transform and invigorate the mind. For Wrytings, the pen is not just a tool, but a conduit for bringing stagnant thoughts into vibrant, fluid expression.

# DISCUSSION QUESTIONS

1. What does love mean to you?

2. How would you define love, and how has your understanding of it evolved over time?

3. What role does trust play in a relationship?

4. How do you build and maintain trust, and how do you repair it if it's broken?

5. How important is communication in a relationship?

6. What are the best ways to communicate openly and honestly with a partner?

7. What qualities do you value most in a romantic partner?

8. Are their certain traits that are non-negotiable for you in a relationship?

9. How do you handle conflict in a relationship?

10. What are some healthy strategies for resolving disagreements and maintaining respect during tough times?

11. Do you believe in "Soulmates or Twin Flames"?

12. Or do you think love is more about compatibility and shared values than fate?

13. What role does independence play in a healthy relationship?

14. How do you balance your own personal growth and space with being in a committed relationship?

15. How do love languages affect relationships?

16. Do you think understanding your partner's love language can improve the relationship? How do you express love best?

17. What are your views on long-distance relationships?

18. How do you maintain emotional connection and intimacy when separated by distance?

19. How does vulnerability impact intimacy in relationships?

20. Are you comfortable being vulnerable with your partner, and how does it influence closeness?

21. What is your opinion on relationships changing over time?

22. How do you navigate the changes that happen in a relationship as both partners grow and evolve?

23. What is the role of forgiveness in love?

24. Can you truly forgive a partner after betrayal or hurt? How do you move forward after a major conflict?

Thank you for reading *Love's Greatest Sorrow*

Nelson Wrytings is an independent author, and his success is largely attributed to word-of-mouth recommendations. If you enjoyed this book, please help spread the word by leaving an online review!